Emotional Journey

Poetry on Love and Abuse

Wriiten and published by: Diane Cheney

ISBN: 978-0-6151-5748-1

Acknowledgments

I want to especially thank my two children, Danielle and Tyler King
for inspiring me in writing this book - They are my heroes.
I have always wanted to have my work published - now it's a wish
come true.
In seeing what I have done they now know that anything is possible
and
that dreams and wishes often come true.

I also give special thanks to my mom for encouraging me to follow
my dreams and for raising me to be just as wonderful as she!

Oh, and of course...another special thank you to the sailor that
put my heart back in one piece - John R. Collier (my Johnathan)

I love you all and God bless!

To all the women and children in the world that have been
abused and to the ones that still are...

There is help out there - never ever give up.

My prayers are with you.

Part 1

Painful past...

Inside My Head

Words
Unspoken
Left unsaid
Buried within
Lost in my head

Anger
Deep inside
Always there
Nowhere to hide

Death
Gone forever
Without a doubt
No use trying
There's no way out...

I Wonder

What is it like to have a smile on your face?
What is it like to be happy?
I was just wondering...
How are you suppose to feel when you are loved?
You see I'm asking because I don't think I'm feeling anything.
Well I was just wondering...
Maybe if I pretend to be happy,
Or force a little smile,
Then I can make myself believe that I am,
But I still would'nt know what it's really like,
So I sit here all alone just waiting...
Waiting for that feeling any feeling to enter my soul.

Fall To Freedom

Standing here
on the edge
alone with my thoughts
with no sound other than my tears
colliding with this rock I stand upon
closing my eyes
leaning back
with one last breath I fall...
smiling
knowing this will be the last
of my pain

Beyond Repair

I no longer had a voice that you could hear
I was invisible to you
yet human form when you slapped my face
with your ignorance
Visible for all of your punishments.

You never failed to find new parts of myself
to destroy.
Most of me has died... parts at a time
Agonizing installments.

What's left is my aching heart
beating in the rythym of decline

Congratulations - you win!

Just a Thought

His words
they take me hostage
What would life be like without him
I often wonder...
When he is gone
will his voice forever haunt me...
hold me back
as if he still existed?

I Await

My home is a giant cage
complete with locks and chains
Desperately wanting to escape
to free myself from confinement
I look for an unlocked door or window
only to be disappointed.

I feel I cannot breathe
suffocating in what little space I am given
One of these days
I will free myself of this cage built for me...

Familiar Face

We have never met
yet I know you all too well
Within your eyes I see your life
past and present
I see the bruises... the ones in your mind
and the ones that have since faded from your skin

Within your eyes
I see loneliness, sadness, and pain...

Within your eyes
I see myself

Display of Loneliness

One lonely bottle upon the shelf
too covered in dust to see its' sparkle
Waiting patiently to be
touched
smelled
tasted
Desperately wanting to be emptied of
its intoxicating substance
Ready to fall
to break into a million little pieces
just to be noticed...
Sometimes I feel this way too

Emotional Wounds

Each scar carved deep within my flesh
represents a time in my life that I felt
angry
lonely
or sad
Inflicting pain upon myself was all I
knew of to numb my emotions
to release the poisons that were slowly
drowning my soul
It was those moments that freed me
from the final dose of poison...
the poison he called love.

If Only You Were Ever Here

I've screamed so much because I needed you...
but you weren't around to hear me,
My eyes cried for all the words I couldn't speak...
But you weren't here to wipe them,
I carved your name into my wrist...
But you weren't here to see the blood,
So I took my own life ...
But you weren't around to hear my last breath...
If only you were ever here.

Sleepless Night

Alone in the dark
the coldness of the dirt
absorbing into my skin
sheltered only by branches
of this tree I lean upon
shivering...
searching for warmth
Will I survive another night?

I Wish...

I wish I were your only addiction...
But I'm not.
I wish that I could protect you from all of the bad things...
But I can't.
I wish you would just listen sometimes...
But you don't.
Sometimes you may think that I'm in your way...
But I'm not.
I'm only here because I love you...

I Fear You

I fear you now
dislike your touch
the coldness of your hands

I fear you now
your words they hurt me
your threats they confine me

I fear you now
that look in your eyes
too scared to sleep

I fear you now
your temper, your strength
that someday you will kill me

I fear you now
and all that you've become
too weak... too afraid
to disappear

So forever I will "fear you now"

Exhausted Soul

Your words were once hurtful
more so than the bruises left behind.
I remember moments when I would hide
from the world, too ashamed to be seen...

Moments I believed that I deserved your abuse
therefore accepting your punishments as if I
were a child taking responsibility for my wrong
doing.

And moments I tried to end it all
just to escape you -
no longer wanting to cry...
to feel pain
So tired of living in fear
and tired of you

Part 2

The happier side of me...

Raindrops

Raindrops
One by one
On my window
Until there are none

Morning dew
On the tall green grass
Drying in the sun
As the rain clouds pass

Sunshine
Fading
Setting in the sky
Beautiful colors
Time sure does fly!

Healing Heart

I once had a heart of many pieces
until one day a beautiful stranger appeared
offering nothing but his unconditional love
In the weeks and months ahead he carefully
stitched thread through each torn piece, using
only his warm words -
On one very special day he confessed his deep
love for me and with that final stitch my
heart was whole

I ONCE had a heart of many pieces...

Then Came You

There was a time I had given up on life
so close to ending it all
no one understood me
there was not one person I could share
my thoughts and feelings with
no one that seemed to care

I had so much to give of myself
yet, no one to give it to
Then you came along
changing my life instantly

Because of you I am here -
You are responsible for all the
happiness in my heart.
It was your concerned attitude
and understanding ways that
captured my entire being.

You gave me so many reasons to continue
on in my journey...
Thank you, for all that you have been
and for doing it so perfectly!

Somewhere Out There

Somewhere out there someone is thinking of you
dreaming of holding you... kissing you
longing to touch you

Somewhere out there someone misses you
your smile... your contagious laugh
the warmth of your skin

Somewhere out there someone truly loves you
wants to prove so, over and over
wants you for all eternity

Somewhere out there someone has given their
             heart
             mind
             body
        and soul to you...

That someone is me - I love you!

Alone With You

I went for a walk today
and took you along

I confessed my need for you...
my love for you
I told you that you meant the
world to me...
that I loved you more than life itself

Though you never said a word
I know you were listening

I went for a walk today
while you sat quietly upon my heart

Definition of Love

Love is not just a feeling
but also a place in which we travel
when we don't want to be alone

A place where everything is known
and understood...
a place where laughter is plentiful...
a place where two people go to share
their souls.

Love is a place that most could only dream of traveling

Define Forever

Is this a "pretend forever"
a fairytale to entertain our souls
something we so desperately want
yet we may never truly have?

A "forever promise" we often make
to create such hope -
to feel secure for the time being?

Or, is "forever you and me" spoken out
of certainty...
knowing that deep within our hearts we
came together to prove that forever is NOT
just a word... a fairytale
rather, something much more

A dream come true...an eternity
an everlasting journey!

Worth The Wait

Some people search endlessly for that
certain someone
while others accept the first someone
that comes along

Is it possible that those in such a hurry
are in fear of being alone?

If only we all took our time
searching the world over
not just for anyone, but the right someone
maybe then our relationships
would last longer

Sometimes

Sometimes I need reminding
that I am wanted, that I am loved
that I have a permanent place in your heart

Sometimes I need reassurance
tell me I will never lose you
that forever we will be

Other times I'll just need your touch
just to feel you close
Am I asking too much?

Yes, sometimes I will need these things...
I hope I'll never have to ask

Keeping My Distance

I'm afraid that someday you will fade away
you will wake one morning realizing
you no longer love me
no longer care

I am afraid of losing you
so I carefully keep one far step behind you
in hopes that if that dreadful time ever comes
my distant heart won't ache so much

Silent Love

Without a word...without a sound
pull me close...hold me tight
lay me down
gently
slowly
touch me, my skin
feel the softness...the warmth
explore every inch
with your hands
your mouth
listen...
to my breathing
my heart beating
each breath
and each beat
is for you
for I live and breath for you
kiss me softly, with passion
kiss my neck, belly, thighs and
my lips...
with your chest upon me, your hands in mine
look deep into my eyes
now... without a word, without a sound
tell me you love me

Bed of Loneliness

Alone in bed
I reach for you
only to find a pillow
holding it so close
so tight
searching for warmth... for comfort
I pretend it is you, this pillow
with my head upon you I cry...
How desperate I have become, for I
have created you from something so lifeless

Silent Friend

Walking by
our shadows collide
for a moment in time
we are one

Souls dancing
  Hearts smiling
    Thoughts entwined

We are no longer strangers
rather two beings whom have yet to speak

Without You

My arms aching
reaching out to you

My eyes tired
full of tears
looking for you

My heart...

　pounding
　　breaking
　　　bleeding

Because I miss you...

Little Sister

If it were possible I would give to you my highest hopes
and my sweetest dreams
If it were possible I would give to you my strength
my happiness, and my life
I would trade my smiles for all your frowns...
I'd do absolutely anything to dry your tears
to end your pain
trade lives with you...
ANYTHING
Just to see you smile

Letter To Mom

To how far you have come
you truly amaze me -

I often travel back in time to the moments you were
so weak, lonely, sad, and afraid
to the moments you felt hopeless and worthless
Yes, I remember those days, those sleepless nights
there were so many...

I remember watching the endless tears flow from your
beautiful, yet tired face.
I never wanted to fall asleep, fearing that by morning
you would be gone... escaping the nightmares -
You never left, not even for a minute. You stayed,
sacrificing and suffering for your children...
with your life in jeopardy you stayed.

Your past experiences have made you the most
wonderful and amazing mom you are today -
Your compassion, courage, and strength will never
be forgotten.

I love you, Mom!